Winter Sleep

by Sharon Fear
illustrated by Peggy Tagel

HOUGHTON MIFFLIN BOSTON

Printed in China

ISBN-13: 978-0-547-01695-5
ISBN-10: 0-547-01695-6

5 6 7 8 9 0940 15 14 13 12 11 10

"Look at the log.
We can sleep in this
log," said the mice.

"We sleep in this log,"
the skunks said.

"Look at the tree.
We can sleep in this
tree," said the mice.

"We sleep in this tree,"
the squirrels said.

"Look at the hole.
We can sleep in this
hole," said the mice.

"We sleep in this hole,"
the snakes said.

"Look at the den.
We can sleep in this
den," said the mice.

"I sleep in this den!"
said the bear.

"You can sleep here,
too," the bear said.

Responding

TARGET SKILL **Understanding Characters** Who are the characters in this story? Tell what they are doing in the story.

Write About It

Text to World Draw a picture of one of the animals in the story. Label the animal. Then write a sentence about your picture.

WORDS TO KNOW

we

LEARN MORE WORDS

den | **hole**

TARGET SKILL **Understanding Characters** Tell more about characters.

TARGET STRATEGY **Analyze/Evaluate** Tell how you feel about the text, and why.

GENRE **Fiction** is a story that is made up.